W9-AOA-091

Cats, Cats, Cats

Cat Care

by Christina Mia Gardeski

CAPSTONE PRESS
a capstone imprint

Pebble Plus is published by Capstone Press,
1710 Roe Crest Drive, North Mankato, Minnesota 56003
www.mycapstone.com

Library of Congress Cataloging-in-Publication Data
Cataloging-in-publication information is on file with the Library of Congress.
ISBN 978-1-5157-0957-2 (library binding)
ISBN 978-1-5157-1123-0 (ebook PDF)

Editorial Credits
Jaclyn Jaycox, editor; Philippa Jenkins, designer;
Pam Mitsakos, media researcher; Steve Walker, production specialist

Photo Credits
Alamy: Juniors Bildarchiv GmbH, 9; Capstone Press, Dan Nunn, 1; Getty Images: Arthur Tilley, 5; Shutterstock:
ajlatan, 17, Alexey Kozhemyakin, 11, g215, 7, Jakub Zak, cover, Jeanine Brouwer, 3, back cover, Milles Studio, 21,
red rose, design element throughout, Stanimir G.Stoev, 19, tarapong srichaiyos, 15, Yimmyphotography, 13

Note to Parents and Teachers

The Cats, Cats, Cats set supports national science standards related to life science.
This book describes and illustrates cat care. The images support early readers in
understanding the text. The repetition of words and phrases helps early readers
learn new words. This book also introduces early readers to subject-specific
vocabulary words, which are defined in the Glossary section. Early readers may
need assistance to read some words and to use the Table of Contents, Glossary,
Read More, Internet Sites, Critical Thinking Using the Common Core, and Index
sections of the book.

Printed and bound in China
PO007732LEOF16

Table of Contents

Cat Care

Cats might act like they can care for themselves. But cats have lived with people for thousands of years. Pet cats trust people to take care of them.

Healthy Food

Cats need healthy food. Protein keeps them strong. Cats get protein from meat in wet or dry cat food. Foods for people such as milk and onions can make cats sick.

Fresh Water

Cats need fresh water.

Clean, fill, and leave out

a water bowl every day.

Many cats enjoy drinking

from a pet water fountain.

Time to Play

Cats need playtime for exercise.

Some cats like to bat balls

or pounce on paper bags.

Leave out toys for your cat

to play with.

Nail Care

A cat's nails need care. Keep its claws trimmed. Give it a scratching post too. Cats need to scratch. They scratch to peel off the dead outer layer of their claws.

Good Grooming

Cats lick themselves to stay clean.

But you can help with grooming.

Brush your cat to keep it from

getting hairballs. Most cats only

need baths if they are very dirty.

Clean Litter

Cats need clean litter boxes.

Scoop out dirty litter every day.

Empty and scrub the box

every week. Dirty litter can

make cats sick.

Safe Indoors

Keep your cat safe inside.

Cats can become lost outside.

They can also get hurt or

catch illnesses.

A Check-Up

Cats need check-ups once a year. The veterinarian checks the cat's eyes, ears, and mouth. They listen to its heart and lungs. Check-ups will help keep your cat healthy.

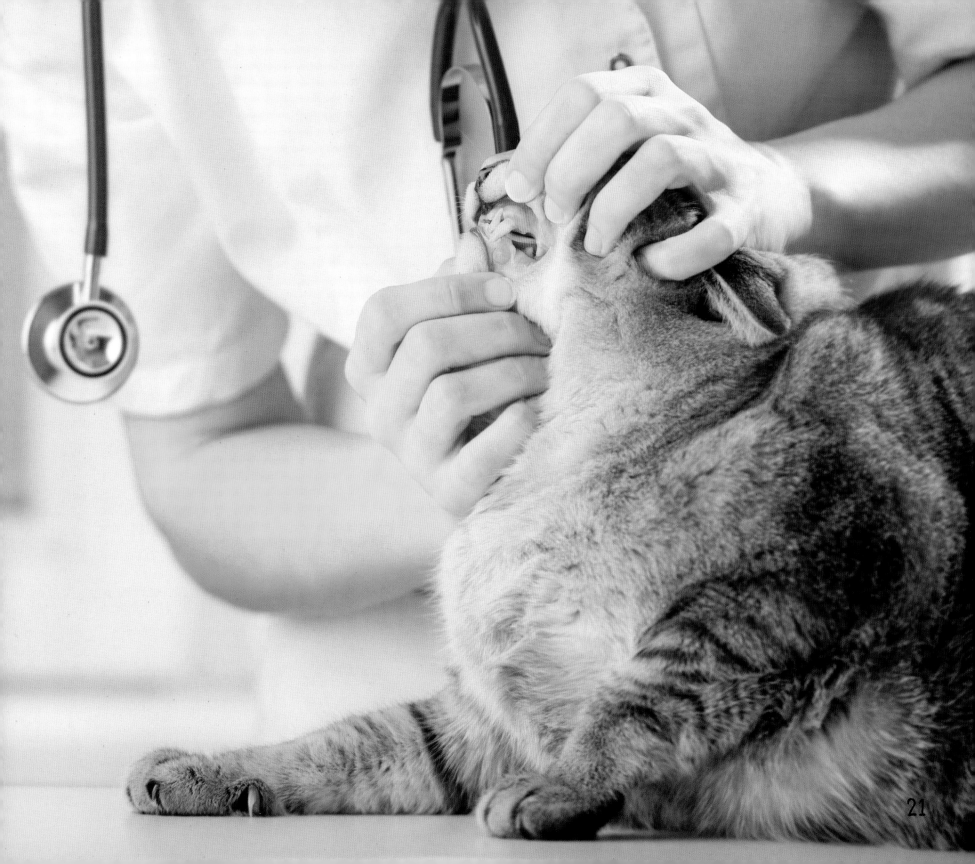

21

Glossary

exercise—moving the body to become strong
and healthy

groom—to keep clean

hairball—a ball of fur that forms in a cat's stomach
after licking itself clean

litter box—a box filled with small bits of wood, paper,
or clay where cats go to the bathroom

pounce—to jump on something suddenly and grab it

protein—part of food that builds strong bones
and muscles

veterinarian—a doctor who takes care of animals

Read More

Ganeri, Anita. *Kitty's Guide to Caring for Your Cat.*
Pets' Guides. Chicago: Capstone Heinemann Library, 2013.

Heneghan, Judith. *Love Your Cat.* Your Perfect Pet.
New York: Windmill Books, 2013.

Hutmacher, Kimberly M. *I Want a Cat.* I Want a Pet.
Mankato, Minn.: Capstone Press, 2012.

Internet Sites

FactHound offers a safe, fun way to find Internet sites
related to this book. All of the sites on FactHound
have been researched by our staff.

Here's all you do:

Visit *www.facthound.com*

Type in this code: 9781515709572

Super-cool stuff! Check out projects, games and lots more at
www.capstonekids.com

23

Critical Thinking Using the Common Core

- Describe one way you can take care of your cat's nails. (Key Ideas and Details)

- Caring for a cat is a big job. What do you think is the hardest part? (Integration of Knowledge and Ideas)

- How often should you take your cat to the vet for a check-up? Why is it important? (Key Ideas and Details)

Index